SUMMER *in* AMERICA

Above: At Ocean City, New Jersey, two old friends sit on the boardwalk.

Opposite: This Rhode Island gazebo, built at the end of a dock, is a perfect place for admiring sunsets.

SUMMER *in* AMERICA

Text by

AMY WILLARD CROSS

Principal Photography by

DUDLEY WITNEY

KEY PORTER BOOKS

Canadian Cataloguing in Publication Data

Cross, Amy Willard, date
          Summer in America

ISBN 1-55013-517-1

1. Vacations - United States - History. 2. United States - Description and travel.
3. United States - Social life and customs. I. Witney, Dudley.
II. Title.

E161. C76 1994   306.4'812'0973   C94-930382-8

Key Porter Books Limited
70 The Esplanade
Toronto, Ontario
Canada M5E 1R2

Distributed in the United States of America by
National Book Network, Inc.
4720 Boston Way
Lanham, MD 20706

Design: Scott Richardson
Electronic formatting: Peter Maher
Archival photo research: Diane Hamilton
Printed and bound in Italy
94 95 96 97 98 6 5 4 3 2 1

*Opposite: A boy studies
his newly captured frog
at a farm in
Pennsylvania.*

CONTENTS

A day at the beach usually ended in sunburn somewhere or other. Before the invention of sunscreen, people used any cream at hand, hoping that spreading it on thickly would keep the sun at bay.

8

Opposite: The carousel at Asbury Park, New Jersey. Generations of children have begged for rides on merry-go-rounds, and then fought over their favorite mount.

AMERICA'S CHILDHOOD

SUMMER IS AMERICA'S CHILDHOOD. FOR THREE MONTHS EVERY YEAR, the whole nation reverts to a younger stage of life. Adulthood is torn off, responsibility and maturity tossed to the floor in a wrinkled pile, and we become as children. Children without worries. Children chasing only after fun, and the phantom bell of the ice cream truck. Children hungering to experience the whole world—and who know only by touching. In June, the childhood joy of getting out of school spreads to the entire country; it's as if the shopkeepers and business people are singing under their breath about no more pencils, no more books.

As it is for children, play becomes our work during the summer—and is practically a full-time occupation. Summer play for adults may take different forms as boats and fishing rods replace balls and bats, but nevertheless it adopts all the seriousness of work. Like recess, it's a time to be outdoors—a short break between exams and homework, an explosion of physical exertion between airy mental tasks. Boys chase the girls, and girls chase the boys. It's let's pretend: we play at being farmers, cowboys, and go into deep country like Crockett or Boone. We amuse ourselves, enthralled in a magical world of one, or we play with others. And although it seems simple, both the play of children and the play of summer are not without purpose. Playing is a way of

West Virginia's famed White Sulphur Springs Hotel, depicted here in 1857, was a summer meeting site for Southern gentry before the Civil War. Colonials came here in the late eighteenth century to take the mineral waters at spring houses such as the gazebo on the left.

learning about the world. It develops the imagination and nourishes the spirit, and makes both children and adults grow.

As the country has matured, so too has its summertime childhood. In the early years of the country, summer happened, business as usual. But eventually, as increasing prosperity let us leave our work, summer turned into the flip-side of the national dream. Now, the values of hard work and achievement which drive the culture are balanced by an embarrassing light-headedness and frivolity come the warm weather. It's freedom—and we dive, swim, and splash in it. And it seems we can do what we want.

For those of northerly climates and Protestant-formed consciousness, summer is a state of mind; the change in seasons does not affect Mediterranean peoples the same way—they just slow down as the heat rises. But here, in America, summer invites a state of abandon—a leaving of things undone, a rare tantrum of indulgence. For three months of the year, we take off, cool out, sit back, and idle the engine that drives the country, because no machine, no matter how efficiently designed, can run all the time. That three-month respite might explain why the machine works so well the rest of the year.

Summer as leisure arrived relatively recently on the American scene. In the

The bathhouse at Warm Springs, Virginia. For almost two centuries, Southerners have sought the springs' recuperative powers.

country's agrarian past, summer was a season with its own special chores—haying, and harvesting, berrying, and canning. Of course, there were also festivals, but these lasted but a day or two. Back in 1772, in Virginia, settlers organized outdoor fish feasts and barbecues; the men and boys went fishing in the morning, and the guests gathered by the riverside for dinner. But people of the era rarely traveled; journeys in dusty, rattling coaches amounted to arduous work and were not relaxing. Still, the upper classes of the late eighteenth and early nineteenth centuries may have made their way to the springs of West Virginia or Pennsylvania; indeed, Washington Irving wrote the life of Washington while renting a house at the Virginia springs. Or the gentry might have driven to the Jersey shore for sea bathing. At both types of destinations, health, not fun, was the primary goal.

The tradition of summer leisure grew as cities did; the explosion of summertime resorts and diversions peaked in the last few decades of the last century. America had become affluent. The cities, which had grown fivefold, had become uncomfortable, hot, unhealthy, and smelly places that needed getting away from in the summer. To fulfill this need for flight, hotels, cottages, and camps were built in watering spots all over the country.

This open-air bus carried travelers to the Adirondacks in the first decade of the twentieth century.

Amusement parks, beaches, zoos, and city parks offered fun to people who could not leave the city.

Still, the vacation, a fourteen-day mandate of rest and pleasure, came off the assembly line, the product of an industrialized nation. Between 1850 and 1950, the manufacturing work week shrunk from sixty-six hours to forty. Less working time obviously resulted in more free time. Gradually, the idea of leisure lost the taint of idleness so detested by the Puritans and got dressed in language of moral necessity. In the last few decades of the nineteenth century, magazines and mavens had to convince Americans that a vacation nourished both the mind and the body. White-collar workers needed to rest their brains from their taxing duties. Around the turn of the century, *Ladies Home Journal* advocated that even housewives needed a vacation, and "should occasionally have a respite from the thousand and one perplexities of housekeeping. That respite may be brief or long but a respite there should be."

Yet, although clerks and bureaucrats enjoyed vacations, labor had to wait the longest to have mandated breaks from work; the holiday wasn't really universal until after 1920. Even then, time off had to be explained. People had to be talked into it. A 1921 article entitled "The Nose and the Grindstone" declared that the man who works hard "deserved many and long hours for

TARRANT'S SELTZER APERIENT.

We never travel without it!

Going away required packing and planning for every possible situation, including stomach upset brought on by strange food and water. In this 1890s advertisement, a woman packs a stomach medicine in her large trunk.

play." Besides the fun he might have, it benefited the functioning of the larger machine: "the professional or business man ... knows that if he takes three weeks off, the result of his whole season's work is better." Making that vacation physical was just as important—the article went on to say that a few weeks of golf a year would conserve that businessman's health. Since then, all those notions have been accepted, and summer leisure has become something we all share, as universally as childhood itself.

Summer meant getting away from daily life, and usually entailed a voyage of one kind or another. Some people went out of town; others ventured to the end of the road; some just stayed at the pool. Young Americans went to camp. People who left the farm for the city often returned to the country for their vacations. African-Americans who had migrated to the North joined their families in the South during a vacation they called a homecoming. City people flocked to the countryside, to the lakeshore, or to the beaches to escape the heat and dirt of town. By the 1920s, many Americans went on sightseeing trips, taking in the natural views and historical attractions. In any case, they went off looking for the pleasure and ease of summer, and stopped wherever they found it.

This family car was abandoned beside a beach house in North Carolina's Outer Banks in favor of surfboards and sandals. The fish over the garage substitutes for a street number.

14

Opposite: The bicycle has always been a good way to tour through summer. First introduced in the late nineteenth century, biking has served as both sport and transportation.

GETTING TO SUMMER

IN THE EARLY YEARS, SUMMER TRAVEL WAS ONLY FOR A SELECT FEW who could afford to book passage by expensive carriage or coach. But summer tourism grew as transportation did. After the 1830s, steamers and railroads started bringing masses of people from the city to the country, and more Americans were able to get away—to a summer in the country. Besides being cheaper than stagecoach, these forms of transport were more comfortable, so traveling was no longer unpleasant. The early trains and steamers dropped off vacationers at the doorsteps of newly formed pleasure oases—resort towns. In these fertile spots, hotels and resorts grew up, usually nourished by a cooling body of water, or at least a view of it. Steamers brought guests to Nahant in Massachusetts as early as the 1830s; they also went up the Hudson and the Atlantic Coast. For almost a hundred years, steamers brought people from the cities to vacations; they still shuffled across the Great Lakes, bringing summer people from Detroit and Buffalo to Chautauqua Lake in New York, as late as 1910.

However, summer vacation spots would never have been colonized without the train. The tracks drew themselves into the countryside, opening up new territories for Americans to visit. As early as 1833, the Mt. McGregor and Lake George Railroad brought holidayers to Saratoga Springs. Some forty years later,

The Nahant Hotel was one of America's earliest seaside resorts. Bostonians traveled across the Bay to stay at this small hotel, where they amused themselves with fishing, shooting, and playing billiards.

tourists could venture west on the transcontinental railroad. Not only did the railroad companies bring people to the summer resorts, they often planned and developed summer towns, building hotels at the end of the line where trains deposited the passengers. Closer to home, railroad companies developed amusement parks—popularly called trolley parks—where their tracks stopped at a beach.

With so much at stake, the railroads often helped promote tourism to far-off destinations. In the nineteenth century, they frequently published travel brochures that encouraged people to holiday at the end of the line. The 1884 *Mountain and Valley Resorts on Picturesque B. & O.* advertised the resorts at Deep Park and Mountain Lake Park in Maryland; Berkeley and Harper's Ferry in West Virginia; Shenandoah Alum Springs and Orkney in Virginia. Orkney, where the hotel accommodated 800 guests, was described this way: "During the season the place is almost a small city, so lively the general appearance, and so large the number passing about. The altitude is such, nearly twenty-three hundred feet above the sea, as to insure the freest play of fresh and balmy breezes and at night lead to slumbers deep and recuperative." The railroad also stressed the fact that the town was reached by daily mail and had a telegraph office, since travelers wanted to get away, but not disappear from civilization.

Trains carried travelers across the countryside in high style. Dining cars on deluxe trains, such as this cross-country train, were outfitted with silver, tablecloths, and even chandeliers.

Train routes expanded farther and farther and the cars themselves became more luxurious. By 1869, tourists could cross the country on trains that offered Pullmans, sleeping cars, dining cars, and observation decks. The train itself was always an adventure, a hotel on metallic wheels that rumbled and rocked on its tracks. There were hallways to wander—just like any boardwalk—and other passengers to gawk at. Even the movement that made eating in the dining car a difficulty was somehow amusing in its distortion, like a funhouse mirror. Summer was always just a train ride away, until the automobile jumped off the tracks.

Just as the train introduced summer grounds to city dwellers who arrived en masse, so did the car. The ultimate American vehicle, the car amounts to a declaration of independence—a four-wheeled manifestation of the individual's rights. Summer travelers could choose exactly when, where, and how they reached their destination. No longer tied to the tyranny of train lines, summer destinations could be located off the beaten track. Roads branched out like concrete tributaries from the steel tracks. Travelers could go even farther afield, spreading out in the landscape, instead of going from one winter city to another summer city. The auto's arrival changed irrevocably the way we spend summer. The Ford Motor Company certainly realized how tourism helped sell

Living on the road is the ultimate in American vacations, and the van represents the smallest possible motorized home. This one was parked along the Texas coast near Galveston back in the days when cars were allowed on the beach.

the automobile, and published *The Ford Treasury of the Outdoors* in 1952 "to help American Motorists get more pleasure out of the recreational opportunities offered by family cars." This paperback compendium of illustrated articles on fishing and hiking, noted, without irony that, since the turn of the century, the machine had increased Americans' participation in outdoor activities.

Not only could they come and go when they wanted, but tourists tooling in automobiles could travel farther, less expensively. When automobile travel first took off in the 1920s, there was not much of anything along the roads—those look-alike strips of fast food restaurants and gas bars had not begun to seed themselves like weeds across the continent. Early drivers had to fend for themselves, bringing their own spare tires, tools, and picnics.

Autobummers, as Sinclair Lewis called them, could cover more territory and move at lightning speed across the map of summer. Motoring along at 50 miles per hour compressed the vacation: so much so that, in 1956, a resort in Jackson, Wyoming, offered drive-by tourists a visit at a Dude-for-a-Day Ranch. For $10 vacationers got a horse and two cookout meals, and were shepherded by a cowboyish guide. It was a hurried wilderness vacation, for just a fraction of the price usually charged at a dude ranch.

The hardest part about getting to summer is deciding exactly where to go. Although this sign-post pointed toward Tradewinds, Blue Lagoon, and Sturgeon Point, passing cars were surely tempted to stop for the burgers and fries advertised at the snack bar.

Cars made movement into a destination. Car trips themselves became a kind of vacation—an adventure in a modern Conestoga wagon. With a station wagon and gas at 17 cents a gallon, a family could take a car trip, pioneering over the interstates to see all the sites. Families lit out to "see the country," marking borders and tallying states. It was quite common to take major road trips. One family made a twenty-one-state odyssey in the 1950s, which they called the "station wagon summer." The car was outfitted into a traveling home: clothing drawers stashed into the back, along with bed platforms and mattresses; the glove compartment was packed with first-aid and sewing kits; a cereal box under the dash devoured the trash accumulated after a day on the road. They ate at roadside parks, camped in forest parks, lived a mile-per-hour existence.

More than anything, the automobile brought long-distance travel within almost everyone's reach. Interstates brought the mountains and seashore within hours of the city—and made that escape a day excursion. And they made their mark on summer. Instead of packing trunks for month-long stays, families crammed the trunk for a two-week holiday. The back seat was filled with children, the belongings were stacked high above. The children only had to keep busy, amused, and quiet. The world of the road became the stuff of

Near Manning, South Carolina, in the 1930s, a farm family traveled the old-fashioned way— by horse and buggy—to their destination.

An air conditioner affixed to the door frame transformed this Buick coupe. Appearing first in the 1930s and 1940s, these air conditioners cooled hot autos using outside air drawn into a cylinder, which contained cold water or ice.

games—counting car types, tallying beaver wagons, racing to find the alphabet on road signs. Toy makers devised special car games like magnetized checkers and activity books, which were sold to parents desperate to make it to their destination without too much distraction. Stops at gas stations where cold drinks, and even bathrooms, were for sale relieved the monotony of the long, hot road. Finally, though, the car doors opened into the landscape of summer.

As the automobile replaced the train as a way to cross land, ferries eventually replaced steamers as the way to cross the waters. With automobile ferries, summer travelers could bring the family car on vacation too. Summer was the only time of year most people took a ferry, except for those living on commuting islands such as New York's Staten Island or Seattle's Bainbridge Island. Cars, trains, and planes move people for both business and pleasure, but ferries seem to exist only for vacations. For the most part, ferries bring city people to islands too far away to have bridges to the mainland; everyone is going to the same place to have a vacation, and for that reason, ferries have an urgent, party atmosphere.

In a corner of New England, Cabin Number 7 offered guests the essentials: a screened door for breezes, four walls for privacy, and two chairs for contemplating the view.

22

Opposite: Sometime between the era of the hotel and the motel, cabins provided shelter to summer tourists. Located conveniently along the road, cabins were rented out to people passing through or those who wanted to stay for a short vacation.

THE PLAYGROUNDS OF SUMMER

SUMMER PLAYGROUNDS ARE FARTHER AWAY THAN THE NEIGHBORHOOD park, their amusements more complex than swing sets. Seashore and mountains become the sandlots and seesaws, and we go there to meet with the same playmates at the appointed times. As the city walls seem to grow higher, and the air within sits heavy with exhaust, we choose to play elsewhere—in wide-open spaces where windows are beyond batting range.

The first American playgrounds were mineral and hot springs, where the main occupation was drinking and bathing. Customers chose baths which ran hot or cold, sulphur or mineral. Playing was an afterthought. Later, the resinous pine air was seen as a tonic; South Carolinians traveled to a spot they called Pineland Village; in the Catskills, Pine Orchard overlooking the Hudson welcomed New Yorkers as early as 1825. At the time, travelers spent the night on straw mattresses—loose for the men, enclosed in ticking for the ladies. Often, they ventured to scenic areas with views of the sublime, such as the White Mountains of New Hampshire, or Niagara—there was even a saying "See Niagara First" to remind Americans that New World scenery deserved a look before journeys were planned to the Old World. The seaside was another popular destination. Before the Civil War, the first major seaside resorts were Nahant in Massachusetts and Cape May in New Jersey, and later Maine. Whether at the

Wives wave handkerchiefs at the "husbands' stage" in this 1882 engraving of the view from the Grand Hotel in the Catskills of New York State. The men returned to work in the city while the women and children stayed behind to spend the summer in the healthy mountain air.

springs or on the coast, these summer playgrounds resembled towns—they were, in fact, outposts of civilization overlooking beautiful views. Each city seemed to have its own resort: Philadelphians ventured to Atlantic City, and at one point, Long Branch, New Jersey, was called a marine suburb of New York.

However, between 1870 and 1920, when the urban population grew fivefold, the recently transplanted population longed for nature. As cities grew denser and uglier, people needed to escape to nature—not untamed, wild, powerful nature, but a pleasing middle ground where they could take their comforts surrounded by a big, beautiful view. Like spring water, sea breezes, and pine-scented air, nature itself was seen as a cure for the ills of urban life. People started to venture into the Adirondack Mountains, into the Poconos, the Catskills, along wild Maine lakes, and some Americans seeking nature even headed north into the Canadian woods. Midwesterners wandered up the mitten of Michigan, into Lake Huron and Lake Superior, around whatever lakes provided shade and shelter. Summer was the time to leave the city, to find nature—or at least a leftover piece of it. And so Americans ventured back out of doors, blinking their eyes, unaccustomed to the searing bright light. And even when they could not leave the city, they sought the solace in nature at botanical gardens, zoos, and municipal parks.

At Hotel Cape May in New Jersey, hotel guests of all ages sat on the shady verandah where the best seats overlooked the surf. In the early years of this century, porch sitting was a preferred sport, and hotel guests practiced it several times a day.

In seaside towns such as this New Jersey resort, hotels and boardinghouses crowd the shore. The Shore-View distinguished itself from its neighbor by a planting of brash annuals.

Mostly, Americans have flocked to the water—giant wading pools where the whole country could cool off. The 1914 book *American Holidays* noted: "For the summer holidays, America is equipped with two of the very best oceans and in addition, she is furnished with most of the fresh water in the world." The rivers and lakes were like "dew on the great countryside," and also enticed vacationers. Resorts and summer communities thrived along the shorelines of lakes and ponds all across the country. The Atlantic and Pacific coasts became long ribbons of playgrounds that filled with people during each summer.

Summer meant getting away, even if just for an afternoon, exchanging the workaday, dollar-a-day world for one of pleasure and fantasy. So Americans got to a world of their own making, tracing fingers on a map until finding a place where there's enough room to wander, play, and shout. Summer's destination could be a resort, a cottage, a campsite, an r.v. parked in a farmer's field, or a houseboat that shuttles between two locks of a canal. Summer could even be celebrated closer to home, at a park, boardwalk, or city beach—somewhere where business is banished and a tie looks out of place. What matters is that the place be dedicated to fun.

Mohonk Mountain House, a grand hotel in Upstate New York, has been popular since the late nineteenth century when it was a hotbed of new ideas—and some old ones. At this progressive resort, no smoking or drinking was allowed. The original owners, the Smiley family, ran seminars on the "native question" and were early conservationists.

Resorts and Hotels

From just about the very beginning, Americans have gone away in the summers. As early as 1795, there was a log tavern for visitors at Saratoga Springs in New York. Cape May, New Jersey, opened its first hotel, The Congress, in 1816. White Sulphur Springs in West Virginia invited invalids and other health seekers to stay in their modest cabins. However, early nineteenth-century hotels were not exactly deluxe: a visitor at White Sulphur Springs noted that guests had to bribe the staff to get any meals.

Although the first resorts were built in the European tradition of Bath, American resorts also sprang up at scenic spots or by the coast to catch sea breezes. Like the springs, seaside resorts also promised health—sometimes in the form of hot salt baths. Salt air and ocean breezes were seen as curatives, which inspired the creation of seaside resorts such as those built on New Hampshire's Appledore Island or Block Island in Rhode Island, beginning around 1850. The Appledore Hotel advertised that a stay on the island matched the tonic effect of a sea voyage: it was supposed to be good for invalids or those with chest and respiratory diseases.

A vacancy sign looks beautiful to car tourists, especially late in the day. The Hi Desert Inn in Nevada points the way with a big lighted arrow.

The hotel was a middle kingdom between the city and the wild. Although surrounded by nature, summer travelers also needed the comforts of civilization. The Catskill Mountain House was an important early hotel, created in 1824. Perched on a shelf above the Hudson River, the Mountain House resembled a lichen bracket growing from a tree. Just one day's travel from New York City, this hotel was extraordinary for the way it brought city comforts far into the country—something vacationing Americans came to expect. A visitor from 1843 remarked: "How the proprietor can have dragged up, and keeps dragging up so many superfluities from the river level to the eagle's nest excites your wonder. It is the more strange because in climbing a mountain, the feeling is natural that you leave such enervating indulgences below." That observation would apply to hotels and resorts for the next hundred years.

The hotel industry exploded after the Civil War, when a prosperous country had money to spare for vacations. The resorts grew to industrial size to meet the growing demand. Cape May's Columbia Hotel housed up to 600 guests—a capacity which was matched, if not exceeded, by dozens of others. The Union in Saratoga filled one city block and had a tree-shaded garden in the back. The smaller hotels often grew outward, adding wings on either side which were

The Grand Hotel on Mackinac Island, Michigan, was famed for its marathon-long porch, which has remained unchanged for nearly a century.

Hotels catering to tourists opened wherever there was scenic terrain. The Sierra Mountains were a popular vacation spot for San Franciscans. In 1906, guests posed for this photograph outside Hotel Sierra in Loyalton, California.

lined by a long verandah. The verandah was always seen as a hotel's prime attraction. Holiday establishments boasted about their verandah's length—often described in fractions of a mile—in advertisements.

Resort hotels were self-contained universes. Hundreds of families slept under one roof, took meals together, went on rides, and danced at the frequent hops. The resorts served up the American plan, three meals a day plus room. Before the Civil War, the Catskill Mountain House charged $2.50 a day; children and servants paid less if they ate at the children's table. The women and children stayed for most of the summer, and the men joined them on weekends or for shorter stays—they would have been bored by the idleness.

For the most part, there were few activities beyond family life; there was swimming, taking the waters, driving, some archery on the lawn, but none of the sports now associated with summer. The main activity took place on the porch, or piazza as these porches were called. Guests took promenades under its shade or sat in rockers and visited. Sociability, meeting and making friends, was one of the primary functions of these hotels. Courting was another summer activity; at Saratoga there was a courting yard, and the Virginia springs hotels had a tradition of serenading a beloved. However, hotel guests wanted to make sure they were with like kind, and to insure this, some

Opened before the turn of the century, the grand Hotel del Coronado near San Diego starred in the film Some Like It Hot.

establishments insisted on references. Social separation continued in the summer. At first, the boardinghouses and hotels of the Catskills would not permit Jewish visitors, but ironically that area grew into the Borscht Belt, filled with resorts such as Grossingers. African-Americans founded a few resort towns of their own, such as Idlewild, Michigan.

As American leisure became more sophisticated so did American resorts. Billiards and shuffleboard were not enough to keep guests entertained. Newly popular sports were added to the hotels' attractions. The Greenbriar at White Sulphur Springs added a golf course in 1884, and other resorts followed suit with tennis courts, sailboats, canoe rentals, and croquet lawns. The turn-of-the-century Hotel del Coronado, a grand hotel near San Diego, even offered a twice-weekly rabbit hunt on their varied menu of leisure, which included tennis, sailing, golf, and archery.

However, while not everyone could afford the high rates of hotels, most managed a vacation anyway. Many families stayed at boardinghouses near resort communities, or they boarded with local farmers, as was common in the Catskills. The Catskills had become such a democratic summer playground that by the 1880s some 70,000 people visited each summer. Many more people were having vacations and needed an affordable place to spend them. The

The Hotel del Coronado in 1928.

32

A postcard of the hotel's tent city.

Painted skulls decorate a western ranch house constructed of logs.

Hotel del Coronado offered luxury to a select few, but since many other people who couldn't afford their luxurious rates yearned for the same resort experience, the hotel had the insight in 1900 to open Tent City, a resort for those of modest means. Behind the grand red-roofed hotel, the Del Coronado erected hundreds of striped tents and furnished them, renting them out for 50 cents per day per person. A family of four could stay for a month for $30, and people came from Los Angeles and all around the Southwest for a seaside vacation. There was a plaza in the center which had stores, a restaurant, a merry-go-round, and nightly concerts. There was even a cold- and salt-water plunger, for those who did not care for waves with their ocean water. Only the canvas (and lack of staff) distinguished the experience from that of guests staying at the main hotel.

The resort underwent another interesting transformation out west, as cattle ranches turned into dude ranches. A dude ranch was a cross between an agricultural enterprise and a hotel. There, city people got in the saddle to live the cowboy lifestyle while on vacation. Dude ranches began as working ranches that accepted paying guests in the 1880s and 1890s to help out with expenses. Easterners, who were called dudes, came west to see the wide-open spaces and even helped work the stock—just like the cowboys. Soon the

Dudes head out on a cattle drive in Wyoming. During the summer, this ranch sent its stock to pastures on higher ground. Visitors accompanied the cowboys on the journey, which sometimes required camping out for several days.

ranches got into the tourist business full time, and spread all over the region. There was the Pinon Lodge in New Mexico, the Lone Star Guest Ranch in Nevada, the Lazy RC or Triangle Ranches in Arizona, as well as dozens more.

Eventually, the guests demanded more comforts and amenities, and the ranches became more sophisticated and began to resemble rustic hotels. Besides working the stock, dudes went riding and fishing, or made visits to scenic areas, just like they would at any resort. Some dudes rode off on trips into deep country that were just like cowboys' roundups. Despite their similarities to eastern resorts, dude ranches always maintained a different atmosphere: at the Neversummer Ranch, there was a smokehouse where guests could smoke their own trout, producing an edible souvenir. During the Second World War, when gas rationing made it impossible to travel out west, dude ranches opened on the east coast to give vacationers the same riding, outdoor experience, even if the vistas weren't quite as large. Wherever it was, the dude ranch offered a glimpse of the great American frontier and the myths of the West.

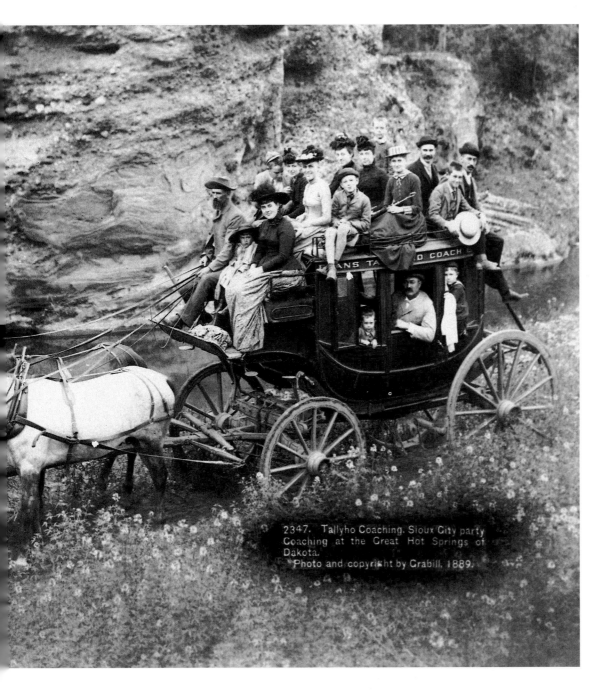

2347. Tallyho Coaching. Sioux City party Coaching at the Great Hot Springs of Dakota.
Photo and copyright by Grabill. 1889.

Dude ranches were popular vacation spots for the entire family. While there, children could play real life cowboy, and dress for the part.

In 1889, these vacationing Sioux City families took a coach ride at the Great Hot Springs of Dakota.

A grand old shingled cottage on the New Jersey shore accommodated a large clan and many friends.

THE COTTAGE

The cottage has long been the headquarters of summer leisure. For many American families, summer meant another home to call their own, a home sweeter than the one they left behind. Summer houses have been around for a long time. In the early years of the republic, people such as Daniel Webster and Alexander Hamilton maintained separate country estates. Yet some of the first cottages grew out of mid-nineteenth-century hotels, which built little cottages and shacks around the main structure to house the overflow. After the Civil War, when New England was emptied of farmers who could not compete with the highly efficient farms of the Midwest, abandoned farmhouses were turned into retreats for vacationing city people. When even those houses could not fill the demand, Americans began building more houses expressly for vacationing. In typical American fashion, summer holidayers sought more autonomy and eventually built their own cottages at summer resorts, away from the hotels, but close enough to enjoy the social life and well-laid table. They also built cottages along the seashore or log cabins in the woods. Still, these summer places collected in areas where like-minded people pursued

Lighthouses, like this one at Cape Lookout, South Carolina, were part of the summer landscape. After they became obsolete, lighthouse keepers' houses were often converted into vacation houses.

These modernist beach houses on North Carolina's Outerbanks huddle together against the Atlantic winds. Each little cottage offers its best angle to the view, which is always the main event at any beach house.

38

Chores and maintenance ruin too many vacations. That problem was well understood by the man who built this house at Camp Ellis on Massachusetts' shore before the Second World War. He built the place on the condition that nothing was ever done to it. Aside from girding the foundation to save the cottage from toppling over, his descendants have followed his wishes—and enjoyed more leisure hours because of it.

Several generations of a family, plus assorted friends, gathered for vacations or afternoon picnics at summer houses. This family lounges at their summer cottage on Deer Island, Maine, in the 1890s.

In the late nineteenth century, summer houses often accessorized standard clapboard with fanciful ginger-bread carved by local craftsmen.

pleasures of the season, thus creating colonies and communities of leisure which were markedly unlike a working town.

In the last century, more and more people came to spend the summer at a vacation house, and the heyday of the resort hotels passed. Most important, vacation houses became more accessible as time went by. At the religious campgrounds, which were popular during the same period when gilded-age millionaires were building their castle-like "cottages" at Newport, middle-class Americans could also afford very small cottages. These gingerbread structures measured some fourteen feet across and were set just feet apart from each other. Inspired by the success of the campgrounds, developers began cooking up whole new resort towns from scratch to fill the need of middle-class vacationers. One such place of the 1880s, Asbury Park in New Jersey, sold itself on its virtuous proximity to the Methodist camp Ocean Grove. Within its 500-acre limits, Asbury Park offered large lots, electric trolleys, and the first sewer system in New Jersey. The town was secular, but maintained the family atmosphere of its religious neighbor. In the prosperous 1920s, more and more families built or rented places for the summer. Housekeeping cottages could be rented by the week. During the postwar boom, there was another boom in vacation houses and properties. Having a second place became even more

William Randolph Hearst owned an estate in northern California that was comprised of several lodges and houses. River House was used by his guests as a perch for fishing.

41

Summer cottages have always had to struggle with the forces of nature. On Long Island's East Hampton, snow fences become sand fences.

42

Many families spent their summers in rustic cabins. It was a simple, old-fashioned way of life, different from the rest of the year. But no matter where people escaped, housework always followed.

affordable with the advent of prefabricated cottages and trailers that could be parked all summer in the same campground.

Whether the cottage was on the sea, by the lake, in the woods, up a mountain, didn't matter. What did matter was that the same people returned to the same house, saw the same friends, played the same games—at a place that was dedicated to fun and enjoyment of a season. Vacation houses had a continuity that life during the rest of the year did not. The summer house may have been passed down in the family, shared by a group, or rented for two weeks, but it has always been the temple of summer. There, Americans have joyfully practiced the rites of that season: a swim before breakfast, sports in the morning, afternoon naps, reading in the afternoon, a barbecued dinner, and an evening's entertainment on the porch. The summer cottage has thrived because it has been built exactly to the specifications of the season. A simple place that is sociable and accommodating, it became the center of sports and play.

This beach house on a stretch of the Pacific Coast Highway in northern California is set precariously on the cliff. Like every other summer house, it reaches out for the view.

44

Oyster Bay, New York, served as a summer home to Teddy Roosevelt among others. This guest house, with its gilt fish and resemblance to an old ship, merely accompanied a grander house lurking elsewhere on the property.

45

Camping enjoyed an explosion of popularity during the last few decades of the nineteenth century. These campers went to the woods and set up tents, which they furnished with the amenities of home.

CAMPGROUNDS

Americans also created an entirely new way of celebrating summer and practicing religion at the same time. The last few decades of the nineteenth century saw a tremendous growth of religious campgrounds—summer resorts run by the Methodist church. Although simpler and less sophisticated than the great hotels, these religious campgrounds spread the gospel of a summer vacation louder than any bugle. The campgrounds or assemblies which flourished all over North America introduced the Protestant middle class to the leisure revolution by dressing down fun with fundamentalism. Church retreats and Sunday school camps carried on the tradition, mixing morals with amusement, making vacations seem less sinful. It all started during the Great Revival in the early part of the century; frontierspeople and farmers would camp out for a few days in the woods to hear preachers. Gradually, the camp meeting grew into the organized campground. The earliest was perhaps Oak Bluffs in Martha's Vineyard where Methodists first camped out in 1835 for prayer and sermons. As the years went by, more and more people came to the scrub oak grove and pitched neat white tents. The faithful also camped at

A steamer lands at the religious summer resort Chautauqua in 1890.

similar places such as Upstate New York's Thousand Island Park and New Jersey's Ocean Grove, buying their tents and camp stoves from outfitting companies. Families moved in for the summer, or part of it, and spent their holidays attending sermons and hymn-singings. Soon afterward, the tents turned into room-sized, pointy-roofed cottages.

These religious resorts tolerated none of the dissolution (horse racing, gambling, drinking, and flirting) common at normal resorts, but offered a Christian alternative. At Ocean Grove in New Jersey, which began in 1869 and where cottages never replaced the tents, leases were granted only to people of "good moral character." The streets were signposted with Methodist or biblical names—even the lake was called Wesley after the founder of Methodism. At one point, local merchants were forbidden to stock novels or tobacco. Still, there was always some fun to be had, if it were chaperoned and not taking place on Sundays. The idea spread, and churches all around the country created holy oases of amusement where parishioners could come and renew their faith in a natural setting—a fact often stressed in a campground's name, such as Lake Pocono Pines Assembly.

The campgrounds inspired another type of religious summer holiday—the chautauqua. The original Chautauqua began in the 1870s on the eponymous

Camps flourished after the 1920s to introduce generations of urban children to nature. In August 1943, at Camp Farm Rock, a Methodist children's camp, a counselor gives children instructions before they leave on a hike.

lake in Upstate New York. It set out to educate Sunday school teachers, but eventually increased its mandate to enlighten all Christians of whatever denomination who wanted to come. The day was spent attending courses, sermons, reading hours, recitals, and a daily religious lecture. The offerings of 1908 set the earnest tone: "On an Old School House," "Everyday Life in France," "The Romance of Papyrus Hunting," "Our Wounded Friends the Trees," "Indian Corn," "Military Life in Germany," "The Milk Supply of Our Cities." Chautauqua also had its amusements; there was bathing on the lake, a waterslide, boating, and a model of Palestine, complete with Dead Sea and Lake Gennesaret. Yet the town's atmosphere was kept pure: it was free of commerce; respectable students comprised the work force; no steamers were allowed to dock on Sundays; and, of course, the town was dry.

More than just a resort, Chautauqua developed its own culture: the trademark Chautauqua salute, a waving of white handkerchiefs in a fluttering form of applause; *The Chautauqua Daily*, a newspaper which had been published since 1875; and a monthly magazine which listed the lectures, and activities at other chautauquas. The Chautauqua culture was cloned all over the continent; in Iowa, there was Clear Lake; in Kansas, Lincoln Park or Clay County Chautauqua; Maryland had Mountain Lake Park; in South Dakota,

In the late 1800s, after a morning sail, a man reads in his canoe.

there was Big Stone Lake—to name a few. Like the mother chautauqua, all these campgrounds offered sermons and lectures—a vacation of self-improvement. Over the years, some of the tents withered back into the groves, but many such summer towns survived, amputated of their fervor, and became family havens of summer life. The chautauqua idea even went on the road, and traveled to places far from an assembly or campground. Like the fair, the traveling chautauqua pitched its tents outside the towns, and offered a few days of amusement and enlightenment, rather than vulgar amusements.

CAMPING IN THE WILD

Although some people sought to renew their faith, many Americans have sought renewal in nature during the summers. As the country became civilized, people wanted to get away from civilization, and they did so by heading out into nature and camping. Camping has been packed into American summers since the mid-nineteenth century. Early campers headed into Upstate New York or the Maine woods, making lean-to shelters from birchbark and using balsam boughs as beds. It was rough and wild. Campers

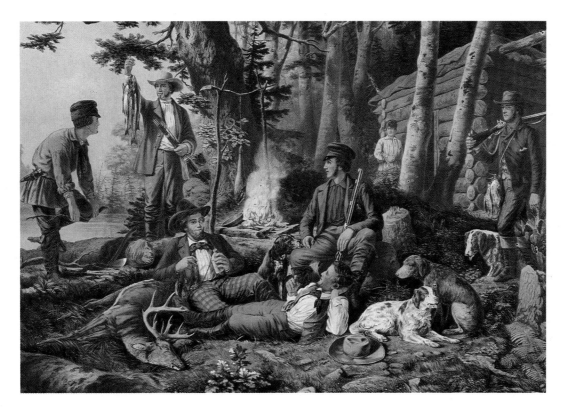

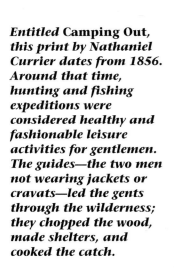

Entitled Camping Out, *this print by Nathaniel Currier dates from 1856. Around that time, hunting and fishing expeditions were considered healthy and fashionable leisure activities for gentlemen. The guides—the two men not wearing jackets or cravats—led the gents through the wilderness; they chopped the wood, made shelters, and cooked the catch.*

went into the wilderness to hunt and fish—living in and living off the woods. The first generation of campers were well-to-do and often hired a guide, who translated life in the woods for city people. But camping took off by the 1870s and 1880s and became more organized; families moved into the woods, living in simple canvas tents that replaced the bark shelters. Some people even brought furniture, and all sorts of paraphernalia to make things easier—and more homey. Fishing and hunting clubs set up permanent base camps in the Adirondacks, around Lake Superior and anywhere within getting-to distance.

Camping was the most direct route back to nature. It still is the best way to leave civilization behind—and it promises freedom, adventure, and the natural world without barriers. And, of course, it was inexpensive. A guide from 1909, *Camping and Camp Cooking,* explained camping's appeal: "The expense of summer hotels and camps deters many and the cost of hiring professional guides prevents others." How-to books helped city people venturing out of doors: that book provided a laundry list of supplies, suggesting campers bring a light tent, ax, camera, kettle, fry pan, coffee can, tight-sealing can for condensed milk, rubber poncho, mosquito net, map, whetstone, rod, reel, cloth bag for use as a pillow, tin plate, cup, and cake soap. To make mattresses, *Camping and Camp Cooking* also advised that campers could buy bales of hay

The advent of the car changed camping forever, making once inaccessible destinations accessible. In 1923, these auto-campers sat on camp chairs admiring the view of Yellowstone National Park from their tent.

from farmers. In that way, camping was an affordable version of the summer vacation: without having to buy land, lease a summer house, pay hotel fees or even club costs—for the price of a guidebook and a few supplies—anyone could have a fresh-air vacation, just like the millionaires had done in the Adirondacks. But every camper, whether a milliner or a millionaire, had to worry about mosquitoes, and every camping guide and camper had a sure-fire recipe for keeping them away:

> Anti-Mosquito Recipe
> 3 oz. pine tar
> 2 oz. castor oil
> 1 oz. oil pennyroyal
> Simmer first two ingredients, cool, and add pennyroyal.

Camping experienced a renaissance in the 1910s and 1920s. It was deemed virtuous. Edward Bok, the influential editor of *Ladies Home Journal*, loathed fashionable resorts for their unnutritious food, artificiality, and late hours, and prescribed a vacation in the woods. Even those who could afford resorts and cottages managed to fit in camping during their summers. Although she had

Trailers were the next step in the evolution of mechanized camping. They were miniaturized versions of the family home, yet despite the trailer's built-in kitchen, most 1950s' campers preferred the campfire for cooking.

two summer homes at her disposal, Eleanor Roosevelt took her sons camping in the 1920s in the Adirondacks and Quebec, as they slowly drove to the Roosevelt cottage in New Brunswick. The experience was seen to be so healthy that camps became institutionalized, so more and more people could enjoy the benefits. Churches maintained retreats where parishioners could come together in nature. Organizations started their own to give people the good-for-you open-air experience; the International Ladies Garment Workers Union had a camp for their members in the Pocono Mountains of Pennsylvania. Even a Pittsburgh department store ran an employee camp in nearby woods—complete with a waterfall for bathing. Unlike going to resorts, camping was ennobling somehow, as a camping article explained: "No man puts himself in a more dignified or manly attitude than when he sits beside his campfire and looks up at the stars."

The campfire functioned as the center of every campsite—the kitchen and the living room. Everyone sat around in a circle on logs, and sang old songs like "Swanee River," "My Old Kentucky Home," "Good Night Ladies," and "My Bonnie Lies Over the Ocean." After a long day of hiking, canoeing, or fishing, the campfire functioned as entertainment; the campers sat around its yellow warmth, watched the stars, and talked until an early bedtime. Then they

clambered into oil-soaked, canvas tents and went to sleep with the smell of smoke in their hair.

However, campfires were eventually put out by modern conveniences. The automobile altered camping for good. First, the car made it easier to get around. As a 1926 article explained, "The automobile will take you out of doors and will give you a new idea of what your country is like." The car created a new form of vacation nomadism called auto-camping. Auto-camps opened up along America's highways. Cities welcomed these tourists; many ran their own motor-camps, supplying water, toilets, showers, barbecues, and even dance rooms practically for free, to encourage campers to pass through town. Even Manhattan Island had a public motor-camp. In the era of the engine, campsites began to resemble urban life more and more. Cars began to pull trailers—land yachts or Pullmans of the road—which were fitted with table, stove, and sleeping accommodations. In a country of constant movement, it seemed right that the summer destination was movable. Camping out imitated the nomadic open-air life, except summer campers grazed on pastures of leisure.

In the early days of Yosemite National Park, before trains came right into the park, visitors could only get there by horse, and had to rough it in order to enjoy the scenery.

Summer picnics and parties often entertained the revelers with absurd games such as this "fat man's race" held at Colorado's Pike National Forest in 1916.

Parks

Parks were the great summer playgrounds—wide open spaces set aside for the common good. President Ulysses S. Grant signed the first park into being, creating Yellowstone in 1872. Niagara and the Adirondack state parks followed in the 1880s. The first parks were intended to preserve scenery and wildlife, but later enlarged their mandate to include recreation. Suddenly, the government took responsibility in helping its citizens get the most out of their leisure time. More and more states and the federal government set aside parkland where urban people could discover nature and the country's wilderness past. Ever since, seeing the country meant visiting these preserved places such as the Grand Canyon, Old Faithful, the Grand Tetons, Mt. Rainier, and Mammoth Hot Springs.

These nature preserves became large summer amusement parks, catering to the summer tourist. Trains often brought vacationers right into parks: Yellowstone was reached by train some ten years after it opened. Along with trains came hotels—great big lodges of unbarked trees and luxury. Even Death Valley had a hotel, called the Furnace Creek Inn. At Glacier Park, Blackfeet

A visitor to this wooded park stops to pin a sprig of wild honeysuckle on her partner's lapel.

56

The Old Faithful Inn in Yellowstone National Park is typical of western resort architecture. The building, from inside to outside, was crafted completely of logs and local stone.

Indians camped out behind the hotel, providing visitors with "a real taste of the West." The national parks were made so amenable to tourism that Rudyard Kipling called Yellowstone "ghastly and vulgar." Although some travelers stayed at the luxurious hostelries, many more camped out, parking their trailers or pitching their tents in sites with water and toilets that were neatly maintained by an army of rangers. Hardier types left the camps of civilization and went hiking, or riding into the open space of the parks.

The national forests were also used as parks, and had a mandate for recreation as well. And Americans accepted the invitation to use the forests for recreation; in 1930, the Forest Service counted 1.9 million campers passing through its lands. At the time, vacationers paid just a dollar a day for meals, sleeping accommodation, recreation facilities, and supervision. Every citizen had a right to enjoy the leftover land. The national forests even leased land for cabins. In the 1930s, *Reader's Digest* reported that 13,000 homes stood in the national forests. Vacationers could lease a fraction of an acre for $15 to $25 a year, if they spent just $500 on improvements or built their own cabin and spent just fifteen days there each year—a length of time equal to the normal vacation. Little summer communities formed in some of the forests where the same families returned to their small cabins summer after summer.

Kids at camp suffered both swimming lessons and swimming races in cold water. At this camp in New Rochelle, New York, campers watched a swimming race from a small boat—in the days before wearing lifejackets became mandatory.

CHILDREN'S CAMPS

If adults had vacations while camping, children received education when living in the outdoors. After finishing the school year, children shipped out for camp. The first camps for children were established in the 1870s, but they really exploded in the 1920s when thousands existed across the country. Boys' clubs, YMCAs, Boy Scouts, Camp Fire Girls, municipalities, and church groups ran many such camps along the shores of lakes. These woodsy institutions often had Indian-sounding names, such as Camp Owatka or Camp Manataka. Many cities maintained camps to continue the education of their junior citizens; Los Angeles had six camps in 1930, four of which were on mountain land owned by the National Forest Service. The experience was seen as so necessary to children's development that many "fresh air funds" helped raise money to send disadvantaged children from the city to camp.

Going to camp was seen as wholesome recreation for children. Kids needed the vitamins of nature, as clearly as they needed milk. And just as milk built bones, camping was seen to build character. A YMCA guide from 1929, *Camping and Character*, declared that camp did just that. It was supposed to

The campfire was always the heart of any camp. Here, at New York State's Camp Nathan Hale, campers sit on crude benches around the fire.

59

60

counteract the degenerating effects of city life by teaching children love of nature, virtue, simplicity, and self-confidence. School may impart mental skills, but camp offered a moral and physical education. It encouraged cooperative behavior, relied on peer discipline, and liberated children from "undue parental affection and domination" (that meant primarily mothers). Many reformers thought women were sissifying the American boy, who was no longer a barefoot kid who spent his afternoons fishing, but an urban creature who had lost touch with nature and needed more character.

To build this character, campers worked hard at sports, at games, and even at nature. Boys, and girls too, learned woodscraft—how to get along in the woods—skills which would do them no good in the city. Although campers sometimes went on overnights, most of the time they stayed at the rustic base camp, where they shared cabins with several others. Life was scheduled down to the quarter-hour; the day began with reveille, dressing, bedmaking, breakfast, cabin cleanup—and sweeping the hard-packed dirt outside. Activities such as archery or maybe leathercraft filled the morning, then came lunch, siesta, and another afternoon activity—sports, swimming, or perhaps a nature walk along a well-marked trail that noted every species of tree. Some camps even booked time for kids to write home to their parents. And, of

A fountain in New York City's Central Park.

course, each achievement merited a badge or stripe.

Later on, camps added more sports, or specialized in one skill or another, but the experience remained the same. Kids still cried for the first few days, short-sheeted each other's beds, and hid whatever candy they received in the mail. Counselors seemed like demigods who were moral, courageous, honest, and more than human; they were admired for their skills in the canoe, and their knowledge of the woods. And the stay at camp ended with the same reluctance with which it began, as fast friends had to wait all year to see each other.

City Playgrounds

Not all summer playgrounds were far away. People could find the leisure and fun of resorts by making a quick trip to the amusement park or nearby beach. And even inside the city limits, we have always been able to find summer at fairgrounds or on city streets where a fire hydrant can be swiftly wrenched open into a torrent.

Yet summer play was mostly confined to the park. Originally common

On a Sunday afternoon in 1905, people flocked to Chicago's Lincoln Park for a band concert.

After the big thaw, every northern city or town turned the water fountains back on. These boys took a break from their cycling to fill up.

A woman takes a siesta in Washington, D.C.'s Rock Creek Park.

63

64

Even after swimming pools became common-place, people still swam at old-fashioned swimming holes.

In the city, summer pleasures are quarantined to the parks. Yet these democratic country clubs offer just about every form of sport and leisure within their green domains; here, a family heads toward the basketball and tennis courts.

pasture for grazing livestock, city parks have always been summer pleasuregrounds. Young people lay on the grass during lunch time, baring what skin they could. Couples took paddleboats into the pond. Families set their table on a picnic bench under the shade, as their meat grilled on a barbecue. The fountain, decorated with a mosaic of pennies, served as a wading pool. A brass band in the gazebo belted out music with words everybody knew. On Sunday afternoons, everyone walked around as if it were a holiday. Softball games filled up each diamond. Off to one corner of the park was the pool—a concrete oasis where people cooled off and played in the water just like the ducks in the pond. Wet bodies dried to a sizzle on the concrete. This is summertime in the city, where pleasure is accessible to all for the price of a token—plus an ice cream bought off the vending cart.

In some city neighbor-hoods, children opened up the fire hydrants, which acted like indus-trial-sized sprinklers.

66

In the 1950s, go-cart and "Anything on Wheels" contests were popular summer events. Kids of all ages raced bicycles and scooters.

Americans who didn't live near an amusement park waited for the carnival to pass through town. When it arrived in Vale, Oregon, in July 1941, this couple rode the giant swing and managed to touch hands in mid-air.

68

Amusement parks are often as good as their food. Although their signs are usually not to be believed, Nathan's hot dogs are famous; indeed, Coney Island was the birthplace of the hot dog.

AMUSEMENT PARKS

The amusement park was the capital of summer fun. In its early nineteenth-century form, it was called a beer garden—a private park within the city that was dedicated to play and diversion of an entirely artificial kind. Jones Woods, located in what is now Manhattan's East 70s, was perhaps America's first amusement park. In those hundred wooded acres on the East River, people seeking amusement could indulge in bowling, billiards, target shooting, or dancing. Similarly, Philadelphians went to Vauxhall Gardens to enjoy beer, theater, and ice cream. By the end of the century, the beer garden had become the mechanized and citified amusement park, and most large cities had such a park within reach. They rose up with lights and brightly painted signs: Santa Monica Municipal Pier; Crystal Beach, Ontario; Louisiana's Pontchartrain Beach; Chicago's Riverview; Glen Echo in Washington, D.C.; Ohio's Cedar Point and Euclid Beach. Of course, there was Coney Island, the ultimate in honky-tonk fun by which all others were measured.

Going to an amusement park was a vacation—a quick trip to another world that was dedicated entirely to diversion. Without even leaving town, summer

Amusement parks offer their visitors a stomach-churning combination of fast food and fast rides. At Coney Island, a Ferris wheel stands behind the sausage vendor.

fun-seekers could exchange fantasy for reality at these hectic entertainment villages. People crowded into the parks on Sundays—which used to be the only real day off. A train or city trolley brought the crowds directly from downtown. In 1893, the Rochester paper described how going to the parks at nearby beaches was "enjoyable recreation that can be secured at home." In a way, amusement parks were a quick, cheap version of the resort. There, every working person could enjoy a little leisure, and those who wanted to stay the night could sleep at one of the many "excursion houses" that lined the boardwalks. The World's Fairs also had an amusement park packed next door to the more serious exhibits; indeed, George Ferris first introduced his ride at the Chicago World's Fair of 1893.

Instead of offering visitors the bucolic scenery and genteel socializing of resorts, amusement parks lured them with rides and games that were bigger than life. Amusement parks were fantastical places, full of lights and signs, where the buildings were done in Moorish, Chinese, or exotic styles. One place in New Jersey even built a building in the shape of an elephant. Coney Island had a park in 1902 called Dreamland that awed visitors with an explosion of light—over one million bulbs lit up the night. The amusement park was an overwhelmingly mechanized universe, where people played on machines—

RAP YOURSELVES

Hair-raising rides, such as the notorious Loop the Loop at Coney Island, attracted crowds at amusement parks. A sign warned riders in 1903 to strap themselves in securely.

carousels, razzle-dazzles, Ferris wheels, midways, and roller coasters, which were first called woodies. The engineering was part of the fun: the first Ferris wheel advertised its specs to potential customers, stating its height, engine size, and other such information. Atlantic City offered an epicycloidal swing; Coney Island boasted about its Cyclone, which dropped 83 feet. Some nineteenth-century parks had flat-bottomed boats that tore down chutes and then landed in the water. One ride at Coney Island was so popular it became immortalized forever in sausage—the Hot Dog.

Of course, there was food, and entertainment, but everyone came for the rides. Each ride was an emotional high that took passengers up hills of thrill, down chutes of terror, finally depositing them on plateaus of relief. It was sensory overload; there was the rush of air, the touch of skin, bodies in contact; then, the crescendo of nausea, and the sea-legs that wobbled as soon as they touched the ground. Spending a few hours like that made the rest of the world seem far away.

Small cities or towns did not have their own amusement parks, but had to wait for the fair. Fairs were a traveling version of Coney Island, and they arrived every summer sure as thunderstorms. Trailers rolled in the same week every year and set up their fun park outside the city limits. Excitement built

At summer fairs, everything—even eating—turned into a competition. At a 4-H club fair in Kansas, a group of boys raced to see who could eat a piece of pie fastest.

for days, as the equipment was unloaded and put together. Just like the Brighton Beaches and municipal piers, the fair had rides and games: Ferris wheels, bumper cars, shooting galleries, and carousels. The winners at ring tossing or darts walked around carrying their prizes proudly. The smell of hot dogs, popcorn, and cotton candy filled the air. The rides might not be as fast, as tall, as electric as those of the parks, but every kid begged to be taken for the day—hoping it might extend into the night. To a child, the fair was a dream come true, an extravaganza of fun that finished way too soon—just like summer.

Once Americans started looking for summer in their cars, amusement was not always a destination in itself, but was picked up along the road like takeout burgers with fries. Amusement parks were reincarnated into theme parks, which were cleaner, more controlled oases of amusement. In the 1930s, Florida tourists visited Marine Land, which exhibited the first captive dolphins. At Florida's Winter Garden, athletic girls performed acts on water skis. Yet after the Second World War, the rowdiness and tawdriness of Atlantic City were replaced by the more clean-cut fun of Busch Gardens, King's Dominion, Knott's Berry Farm, and Hershey Park.

Tourist attractions also popped up along the ever-increasing number of

Collecting trinkets, whether bought or found, is an intrinsic part of any holiday. In case tourists did not have time to visit the nearby Gulf of Mexico, this shop in Galveston, Texas, lured buyers with sirens and then sold them seashells and knickknacks made from local shells.

highways, beckoning travelers to stop and spend a few dollars at a pit stop of entertainment. The signs were, of course, irresistible to children. In the 1950s, "The Enchanted Forest" in very down-to-earth Maryland lured little Hansels and Gretels from their cars. This park reconstructed the landscape of nursery rhymes: The Three Bears' House, Jack and the Bean Stalk, all came to life. A magic telephone booth connected visitors to Rapunzel, and a slide ended in a pot of gold. Other roadside attractions appealed strictly to grown-ups. Along the road in Walker, Minnesota, U.S. 34 was turned into Handicraft Highway, where craftspeople of all types made and sold their wares—souvenirs such as beaded Indian moccasins. Off highways in every state, pioneer villages, Shaker villages, Hutterite colonies, Pennsylvania Dutch farms, and Sturbridge-type villages provided educational fun and meaning for families driving through summer. These old-time villages were a fantasy world just like Dreamland had been, except their fun hid behind instruction. Besides doling out information on historical plaques, these roadside attractions offered a few moments of delight, a souvenir to take home, and interesting postcards that could be sent to the people left behind.

Like sidewalk artists, seaside sculptors charged passersby to look at their creations before they were washed away.

Generations of children have buried each other in the sand and called the final product sand mummies.

THE BEACH

For people who lived in cities with a lake or coast nearby, summer was as close as the beach, a special warm-weather park where leisure was packaged into one sunny afternoon. By the 1930s, more than 200 cities maintained municipal beaches where its citizens could gobble up all the experiences of summer in just a few hours—swimming, sports, games, and an outdoor meal which had once been called a "shore meal." New York State established Jones Beach on Long Island in 1929. It was intended for people who could drive 25 miles from Manhattan to this beach along Long Island Sound. Jones Beach was purposefully made inaccessible to those without automobiles, and no train lines were allowed to approach. However, in many cities, the trolleys traveled from downtown right to the water, disgorging dry people into the dry sand.

There, the city population lay, horizontal in the shade of umbrellas whose stripes had faded from the sun. They sat on folding chairs to protect their skin from the scratch of sand. Adults were happy to stay still, warming under the rays of the sun, while children built castles, buried each other under sand mummies, and ran into the water, screaming as the waves crashed around

By the 1920s, bathing costumes had taken on a racier look. At Balboa Beach in San Diego, California, these flappers formed a conga line on the boardwalk

Many towns by the beach have run establishments like this one at East Hampton, Long Island. People staying in cottages inland, or those passing through for the day, could rent out bathhouses to serve as their headquarters and changing area.

This Mayan Temple was created for a sand castle competition at Carmel, California.

them. Each family created its own encampment on the beach; towels and piles of city clothes were stacked up like buoys marking property lines and channels, thin easements that let swimmers pass through on their way to the water. Games of volleyball were organized around nets set in the sand. And the lifeguard lorded above it all, in a high chair of authority, a whistle around his neck and little girls loitering at the bottom of the ladder.

The roar of the ocean was sometimes matched by the call of the boardwalk. The great open water drew some people to the beach, but others were pulled with the strength of an undertow to the boardwalk—a wood ribbon of civilization sitting above the sand. The boardwalk offered a variety of unwholesome amusements. In the early days, there was vaudeville and "one-step" dancing, lion tamers, snake charmers, souvenir shops, and eventually even nickelodeons. The boardwalk bustled with life like a city, a bazaar, a souk. Booths, rides, oyster stands, and photo shops lined this hallway of entertainment. The boardwalk was the only place to get salt-water taffy wrapped in waxed paper, which could be washed down with sarsaparilla. A boardwalk was so essential to beach life that even small towns along coasts, such as Lanark in Florida, had their own little promenade. At Cape May, New Jersey, the boardwalk between the main street and the surf was called the

The age of parasols gave way to the Coppertone era in the 1960s. However, even the most ardent suntanner sometimes needed a little shade, provided here by a scrap of clothing.

80

Sea grass on the dunes near Currituck Beach Lighthouse on the Outer Banks, North Carolina.

81

For many years, the beaches of Cape Cod south of Boston, have attracted tourists and beachcombers from all over New England and beyond.

A lifeguard station protected every public beach. The guards were always at the ready with stretchers and lifeboats to save swimmers struck by cramps or undertows.

83

"Ladies' Mile." Walking the boardwalk was a big part of going to the beach, and in between sunning, swimming, and picnicking, beachcombers promenaded down this enfilade of fun and food, buying souvenirs to take back home.

Even inner tubes can take on magical powers in the summer.

Opposite: In the Oklahoma Territory back in 1890, with no sea or lake nearby, a man cooled off his friends' children by hosing them down, fully clothed, in the front yard.

THE PLAYING OF SUMMER

SUMMERTIME IS THE SEASON OF PLAY. IN THE HOT WEATHER, WE WILL make a game of almost anything, playing with whatever comes to hand, if it can be held like a bat or thrown like a ball. Mackinac Island, Michigan, holds a rock-skipping contest every summer. In Cornwall, Connecticut, the otherwise flinty Yankees stage a frog-jumping contest. A century ago, Asbury Park in New Jersey instituted a baby parade—rather than gaudy floats, infants formed the wholesome processional. Some beaches even made sand-castle building into a contest. Besides these organized festivities, there were the millions of games of pickup ball; the aquatic chase of Marco Polo played out in pools; volleyball on the beach; or scavenger hunts that stopped at every house on the lake. From June to August, the nation was, and still is, obsessed with games.

However, in America's infancy, work and play were tacked together; people gathered for corn huskings, quilting bees, candle dippings, and barn raisings. The workers visited as they husked, sewed, dipped, or hammered. There was food, company, good talk, and perhaps even music and dancing when it was all done. Yet once corn meal came from a sack, once blankets came from catalogues, once kerosene gave more light than candles, once barns were replaced by garages, the notion of play became divorced from work. Now the two exist in separate spheres, different axes. Time is neatly divided as well:

86

Tucked away behind the cottage, summer gardens replete with fruit trees and fresh lettuce were a place to wile away afternoons. A picket fence kept deer away, even if it was not white-washed every summer.

One of summer's joys is a garden in full bloom.

nine months are for labor and just three are set aside for playing.

As the practice of leisure spread, games developed to fill the increasing supplies of free time. As more and more people led sedentary lives, they compensated by picking up sports—which served as a substitute for the hardy outdoor life. The height of the vacationing era during the last few decades of the last century saw the introduction of many sports such as tennis, golf, and bicycling. Skating rinks also drew crowds at resorts of the period. Certain activities such as fishing and boating were transformed from normal tasks into leisure. Miniature lawn golf existed as early as the 1920s, and has been a favorite of children ever since. Still, certain games such as horseshoes, croquet, and badminton are played only in the summer—they just don't make sense at other times of the year. Warm weather also enticed people to play on the water—which itself became a playground that welcomed swimmers, boaters, and fishermen and -women.

In the twentieth century, summer play became more active and vigorous. And urban people seeking escape looked to outdoorsy activities such as hiking, mountaineering, and canoeing. Summer playing even created its own institutions — marinas, golf clubs, and casinos. An ancestor of the country club, the casino acted as a clubhouse in resort towns where people played lawn

At a country club, a group in their spanking clean tennis whites warm up before class.

Opposite: On this summer day in the 1920s, hundreds of men and women joined a calisthenics class on the beach at Ocean City, New Jersey.

After sailboats, canoes, and motorboats, came water skis. This water-skier prepares to take off as soon as the motor cuts loose.

At Cape Canaveral, Florida, these trailers formed a summer town of leisure.

tennis and met for socializing. And, of course, the country club later served as a summer headquarters for many Americans living in the suburbs. The main thing was that people with the same interests joined each other in yacht clubs, cycling teams, croquet clubs, hiking groups, as they all played together. Not all such playful institutions were elitist, however; by the 1930s, many municipalities maintained golf courses so that everyone had a chance to putt and drive.

On summer vacations the atmosphere is so playful that even normal daily activities seem less like chores. We even make expeditions to gather food: berrying, clamming, or crabbing counts as an amusement—an outing just like souvenir shopping. What people gather varies from place to place: on Long Island or Nantucket people did, and still do, gather beach plums, which are made into jam, canned, and brought back to town for winter breakfasts. Still, the most difficult job of a summer day has always been choosing which game to play, for how long, and with whom.

Atlantic City was a very popular resort. In the summer of 1910, swimmers and day-trippers packed into the town. Those who didn't want to play in the surf dallied with fairlike amusements on the pier.

First introduced in the 1880s, golf had attracted both men and women players by the 1920s. Here, young women players pose on a Maryland golf course.

CROQUET

No game is quite as summery as croquet. As it requires little real exertion, croquet can be played on the hottest of days on a crew-cut carpet of grass, which is preferably shaded by a generous tree. Croquet is an intensely social game in which competition is second to camaraderie—for those who happen to be winning. It first appeared in American summers in the 1850s. And for the next fifteen years, croquet was quite a craze. Dozens of books appeared to explain the game: one advertised itself as "Croquet as played by the Newport Croquet Club." In 1855, a Mrs. Devereaux published *How to Play Progressive Croquet*; it was a progressive game indeed, for women were allowed and even encouraged to play croquet—with men.

In fact, croquet was one of the first sports or games men and women could play together. Both sexes competed on a level playing field, and the croquet lawn was also a course fit for flirting. Taking a croquet on someone's ball was a way to pay him or her attention, to get attention in return, to start a rivalry, to tease. There was plenty of time for pleasantries between shots. Amorous pursuit could be camouflaged by mallet and ball, and the crooked course

Croquet took off in the 1860s and 1870s. Even women were allowed to play this graceful lawn game, which is portrayed here by Winslow Homer in his painting **Croquet Players.**

became a metaphor for courting. Because ladies' ankles were sometimes exposed while shooting an opponent's ball, and because of the long dalliances between hits, croquet was considered scandalous by some, and the game was banned in Boston in the late 1890s. However, its chic was soon replaced by lawn tennis, another game that men and women played on a carpet of grass.

But like humidity or heat waves, croquet has waxed and waned in the American summer; its popularity revived every so often. Surprisingly, even the very literary members of the Algonquin Club played the game. Wags such as Alexander Woollcott, Dorothy Parker, George Kaufman, and Moss Hart played with a savagery that equaled their wit. Once, some members of that group were playing at a Long Island country house and refused to end the competition at dark, but continued by illuminating the play with car headlights ringing the lawn. As country house lawns shrank into suburban plots, croquet continued in the backyard. It became a family game that everyone could play since it took little skill or fitness, just a desire to get into the spirit of the game. Department stores sold scaled-down sets, with mallets light enough for a child to pick up. With courts laid out between the patio and swing set, siblings shot each other's balls into the bushes and played as dirty a game as they could get away with.

Everybody of every age played baseball. At this turn-of-the-century pickup game, a pillow served as home plate.

BASEBALL

Baseball represents the ultimate American sport. For over 150 years, Americans have played and watched the game with equal passion. Homegrown rather than imported, baseball evolved from one-o-cat, two-o-cat, and the game of town ball, which had four bases. The first game of baseball took place in 1839 in Cooperstown, New York. Within twenty years, there were professional teams, and the ritual of going to the game etched itself into the American summer—complete with hot dogs and waving pennants. Besides watching the game, fans counted it, calculated its averages, and figured its probabilities. Everyone had a favorite team, which they hoped would make it to the World Series.

As much as Americans loved to watch baseball or hear it play-by-play, they played the game themselves just as passionately. Nearly everyone—adult or child, female or male—hit a few balls each summer. Kids played softball at recess and then again during gym class. Companies formed teams and played against one another in the park. Boys spent a good part of their summer practicing and playing for the Little League, back when gender apartheid ruled

Even the smallest town carved a baseball diamond out of available parks or fields. In June 1941, this boy watched a baseball practice in Huntingdon, Pennsylvania.

in sport. More often than not, summer picnics finished with an impromptu game; rocks, pieces of wood, or piles of sand substituted for bases. Still, the best baseball happened in the backyard, where kids cobbled together their own games, without a quorum of nine. Scruffy backyard leagues changed the rules to suit four team members and two bases. No matter how unofficial the game, each line drive felt good and sweet as victory. And whoever hit a ball that flew into the neighbor's yard, and became a homer, danced and shouted as if it were the last inning of the World Series.

On hot days, people flock from nearby towns to the beach. Sometimes it becomes so crowded that swimmers have to use the seawall as a beach.

This swimmer wears an early swimming cap.

SWIMMING

Summer's heat has always had one sure-fire antidote; like fire, it needs to be doused with water. Despite air conditioning, screened porches, pitchers of iced tea, and personal-sized palmetto-leaf fans, nothing refreshes like a swim. Swimming seems to change the body's temperature from the inside out, rinsing salty sweat off the skin with sweet water. Swimming has been the season's main refreshment almost since the beginning.

As early as 1838, floating baths were moored at New York City's Castle Garden—bathers didn't necessarily go straight into the swift-flowing river because swimming wasn't a universal skill at the time. It was called bathing in those days, and was considered as healthful as sea breezes. The natives of Orchard Beach, Maine—one and all, young and old, babes and matrons—came to be dipped into the salt water. This always occurred on July 26—well before the water warmed up or before the air became hot enough to make anyone actually want to go in. In the 1840s and 1850s, New Yorkers traveled ten miles south of that city to bathe at Coney Island. Even late into the century, many people bathed rather than swam: at New Jersey or Nantucket beaches, ropes

Steelworkers' children in Pittsburgh, Pennsylvania, play in a homemade swimming pool in 1938.

were stretched out into the surf so non-swimmers could walk into the water, clutching the towrope like a banister as they descended the continental shelf. Then, as now, a lifeguard monitored the shore, although in the early days a sea captain often performed the duty.

Early summertime celebrants might have had trouble swimming because of the thirty-odd pounds of clothing they were required to wear. The bathing costume worn after the Civil War consisted of "drawers fastened at the ankle, and a tunic made with a yoke, night-gown fashion, reaching to the knee, and confined at the waist by a belt." The costume was sober, in gray, black, or dark blue. Straw hats or mobcaps kept heads modestly covered. Such costumes rented out for the day; the ticket was pinned inside. Gradually, bathing dresses grazed the knees, but were still worn with stockings until the daring 1920s, when hemlines came way up, and women bared their limbs. By then, the dress slimmed down to a suit. Wool was the standard until sometime late in the 1930s. Men also had to be covered up; they wore long wool shorts and tunics that matted their chests down, until the 1930s—the decade when even male bathers lost their shirts. Ever since, more and more fabric has peeled off the swimsuit, exposing more and more skin to water, air, and sun.

Despite the propriety of the uniform, then, as now, people knew the sheer

"Just a Sip at Twilight"
IRON CITY
PILSENER & LAGER
"The Talk of The Town"
Schenley 7400

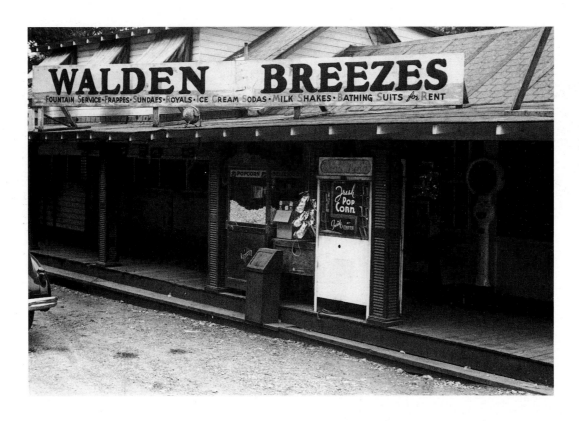

102

deliciousness of swimming in nothingness: at Long Branch, New Jersey, men were allowed to bathe naked before 6:00 a.m. At boys' camps, it was common for the campers to swim nude—a tradition which continued at many YMCAs. (Girls did not seem to enjoy this institutionally sanctioned skinny-dipping.) There was even a skinny-dipping hymn:

Once I went in swimming
where there were no women
down by the deep blue sea.
Seeing no one there
I hung my underwear
on a willow tree.
I dove into the water
just like Pharoah's daughter
floating through the Nile.
Someone saw me there and
stole my underwear
and left me with a smile.

In Northhaven, Maine, boats wait at the dock, like cars outside a shopping mall.

103

Excursion boats take tourists down scenic waterways throughout America. This one, which steamed down the Mississippi, was docked near Red Wing, Minnesota.

Because swimming is such a vital part of summer, vacation establishments far from a shore or sea began building pools as a substitute for the real thing. At Ten Mile Hot Springs in Montana, turn-of-the-century vacationers could bathe in the Natatorium, a huge indoor swimming pool. Filled with water from the hot springs, the Natatorium also had toboggan slides, swings, and ladders for playing in the water. Just about all resorts since then, even roadside motels, lure guests with the promise of a swim, because it's not summer until there's swimming. Indeed, the first swim of the year marks the season as clearly as the last day of school. Eager to turn the page of the calendar, we dive into the water—lakes, rivers, swimming holes, a pond made or created—leaving our clothes on nearby bushes.

BOATING

Come summer, Americans have always taken to boats and played fisherman or sailor atop the water—be it pond, lake, river, or sea. Boats transcend transportation and amount to a relaxing diversion unto themselves. In the nineteenth century, summer people traveled in rowboats—skimming along the

A gaggle of rental boats, each supplied with an identical outboard motor, gas tank, and paddle in case of emergency.

105

Rowboats crowd onto the water of Bronx Lake, New York, on a summer weekend in the early part of the century.

surface, like waterbugs. Yet, by the 1880s, canoes appeared on lakes and rivers in Maine and in many parts of Upstate New York, Michigan, and beyond. The canoe suited the natural landscapes summer travelers craved in the late century, as it could navigate in small rivers and could be carried from one lake to another. Unlike simple rowing, canoeing was a craft that had to be learned; with its various strokes and cuts, it suited people looking for accomplishments in their leisure.

Of course, sailboats have taken the wind and tacked across bays and lakes since the mid-nineteenth century; the New York Yacht Club dates back to the 1840s. Sailors formed more yacht clubs and organized regattas to see who could sail the fastest. Some summer areas became sailing meccas; with good winds and challenging waters, the coast of Maine or Long Island Sound attracted sailing crowds. In places such as the Sound, sailing was practically a religion; boys learned their craft in small catboats, crewed on someone else's boat, and eventually worked up to regattas.

Like many vacationers, Theodore Roosevelt loved spending his days on the water. Rowing and sailing were the "permanent amusements" at his summer home on Oyster Bay. In his autobiography, he lamented the advent of motorboats: "I suppose it sounds archaic, but I cannot help thinking that the

The New York Yacht Club was founded in 1844. In this turn-of-the-century photograph, three people set off in a small launch.

people with motorboats miss a great deal. If they would only keep to rowboats or canoes, and use oar or paddle themselves, they would get infinitely more benefit than by having their work done for them by gasoline." Despite his objections, motorboats replaced rowboats for getting around and playing around on the water—and the rowboat has rarely been seen since.

The 1920s and 1930s saw an explosion in motorboats; boat clubs formed to gather like minds, and gas pumps became a staple of any marina or city dock. After the Second World War, when boats could be manufactured in large numbers, motorboats became the standard of the summer landscape. Just as the car helped spur sightseeing and travel, motorboats opened up more territory to summer visitors and so helped promote the development of islands. And, of course, along with motorboats came waterskiing. Besides boating for sport, summer tourists often saw the sights by boat. Niagara Falls offered a tour on the *Maid of the Mist*; in Florida, glass-bottomed boats such as that at Wakulla Springs let tourists peek down below; cruises operated down rivers such as the St. Croix or Snake; and paddleboats let tourists show themselves the sites.

The magnificent racing sloop, Defiance, sails off the coast of Newport, Rhode Island, in 1914.

108

In Florida during the 1890s, vacationers toured the Tomoka in this well-shaded boat.

109

*Early in this century, a
trio posed with their
prized catch—
a devilfish.*

FISHING

Well before Huck Finn and Tom Sawyer rolled up their pant legs and waded
into the Mississippi with cane poles, fishing was already one of the great
American pastimes. As far back as 1732, a group of wealthy Philadelphians
started a fishing club, and the members (all men) went fishing for a fortnight
each year. Once more Americans had tasted real leisure, fishing changed from a
practical food-gathering activity to a pleasurable pursuit. An 1823 engraving of
the Nahant Hotel in Massachusetts shows men and women standing by the
rocky Atlantic shore, holding fishing rods. In no time at all, fishing was
elevated to a sport, complete with ethics and commercially available
paraphernalia. Fly-fishing, however, evolved into an art; it required the
knowledge of a naturalist and the dexterity of an Oriental rug weaver. Between
1870 and 1901, some one hundred books were published on the sport of
fishing. Like nature or camping, it was seen as a cure for urban life.

    Some people fished for sport, others fished for breakfast; yet, fishing was
part of just about everyone's summer, whether it was surf-casting, trolling with
live bait, or fly-fishing. Kids tried their luck with worms and hand-me-down
rods. Even city folks got out their poles and stood by whatever stream or river

A man walks toward Lake Providence in Louisiana, carrying his fishing poles on his shoulder.

112

Rocking chairs painted shutter green are lined up along the porch of this resort.

ran through town, waiting for luck, a bite, a fight. Victorian women were also known to cast alongside their men. Fishing enthusiasts went on special fishing trips, traveling out west in search of pure trout streams, or they went into far-off natural areas where the fishing was good. Really good catches had their pictures taken with the victorious fisherman, and the prize catches got stuffed and stuck on the wall of a cottage or den at home.

Even the country's leaders fished. President Herbert Hoover wrote a book about it called *Fishing for Fun*. Because 25 million Americans bought fishing licenses, Hoover remarked that any politician who aspired to popularity would do well to take it up—although anyone seeking re-election should have his picture taken with kitchen-variety fish rather than the game species, which did not impress voters. Even more, he noted that fishing was a democratic pursuit since all men are equal before fish. Certainly fishing brought people outdoors, into nature, but its long-standing appeal as an activity is explained by its inactivity. After a winter of work, and a summer full of sports and games, fishing was the only time one was encouraged to stay still. And nothing camouflaged idleness better than a rod.

A Fourth of July afternoon in Hartford, Wisconsin.

SITTING ON THE PORCH

Whether in town or at a summer colony, Americans spent a good part of summer just sitting on the porch. Before the days of air conditioning, the porch was the only room that didn't trap the heat. Sitting on the porch was a way to be outside and inside at the same time.

At nineteenth-century hotels, sitting on the porch amounted to the main activity. Vacationers visited with one another and rocked back and forth in the reed rocking chairs. The verandah was shaded and cool, and the center of all activity. At cottages, summer life also happened on the porch, which amounted to a fresh-air living room. At night cottagers would stay on the porch, hiding behind the screens from mosquitoes, sitting in the dark, and playing parlor games. In the city, the stoop became a kind of porch, where the household could escape the heat inside. Families sat on the steps and gathered to watch the activity outside. Only in summer did people stop to watch the world go by—be it the Atlantic surf or the neighbors in their garden.

Summer is a time for families to get together. Here, a family reunion enjoys a "shore dinner" under the shade.

116

Summer picnics happened wherever there was good scenery. Families set the table on a blanket on the sand, and dined in the fresh air.

PICNICS

Even meals become playful in the warm weather, as we sit down to table on the grass. Having meals out of doors has always been one of the best ways to celebrate the season, and Americans have done it forever in city parks, backyards, orchards, beaches, and on riverbanks. Colonial Americans gathered for fish frys. Floridians used to have something they called bee's teas. Nineteenth-century hotels often organized picnics as outings. Early vacationers would leave their hotels for a drive to a destination known as the local scenic spot—a waterfall or a spectacular view. There, they would unpack hampers of lunch prepared by the hotel kitchen. To have a lunch on the grass, surrounded by nature and other revelers, seemed like an adventure. A picnic could be a vacation itself—an all-day excursion marked only by pleasure. Eventually, the camping craze changed picnics by bringing camp cookery to an afternoon outing; barbecuing the main course over flames became part of picnicking, and just about every American park now has grills within easy reach of the wooden picnic tables.

Picnic food is a celebration in itself. As light-hearted and unserious as summer, the stuff of picnics can be picked up with the fingers. Corn on the

Texans who lived in San Augustine in the 1940s sought sweet relief at the soda fountain in Rushings Drug Store.

Watermelon finished many summer meals, as it needed no forks and the seeds could be used for sport. At this Philadelphia picnic in the 1950s, Howdy Doody presides over a water-melon-eating contest.

cob, watermelon, hot dogs, hamburgers, fried chicken—these are fresh-air victuals, sticky and tasty enough to make even the most polite people lick their fingers. Of course, some picnic foods require the knife and fork of civilization. Just as Thanksgiving needs turkeys and pumpkins, a picnic can't really be conducted properly without potato salad or coleslaw—helped onto a fork with cornbread or biscuits. The whole meal finished with a slice of berry pie, and was washed down with lemonade or iced tea, which have been the perfect beverages for cooling down on a hot day since long before either came from a powder.

All across the country, fireworks explode on the Fourth of July, marking America's favorite holiday with shooting stars of gunpowder.

Opposite: In the late nineteenth century, Asbury Park, New Jersey, staged a baby parade. The mothers wheeled their charges in front of hundreds of spectators.

THE FOURTH OF JULY

7HE COUNTRY'S CHILDHOOD CULMINATES IN A BIRTHDAY PARTY, AND
the Fourth of July is America's collective celebration. Just as children count the
days until their birthday, the entire country looks forward to Independence
Day. On the fourth day of the seventh month, everybody—no matter where,
no matter who—celebrates the birthday of a document, the Declaration of
Independence, pen on paper that has lasted over two hundred years. For the
most part, the day has been marked with a picnic—be it a church social, a
neighborhood picnic, or just a friendly potluck. Along with the food—hot
dogs and corn on the cob, potato salad, and all the rest—there were fun and
games special to that day. Often the celebrations included a track meet, or
more light-hearted competitions such as three-legged races or egg-throwing
contests. The ladies went at each other in bake-offs, competing for the best
blueberry crumble or apple pie. Some towns held a parade. Floats, majorettes,
the town's oldest citizens, and temporary queens paraded down main drags,
accompanied by veterans who were as decorated as wedding cakes.

The day reached its climax when the sky lit up with pyrotechnic
explosions. Like the candles on a cake, fireworks were blown out with one
great hurrah. Families set off Roman candles and schoolhouses in the
backyard. Before the fun stuff was outlawed in the mid-1950s, kids had their

Parades often punctuated summer's end with a full stop. In 1941, a marching band and a company of clowns assembled for the Labor Day Parade in Silverton, Colorado.

Fourth of July festivities began in the early afternoon and ended late at night. Celebrants always suffered from too much food, drink, and excitement. Two tired picnickers take a break from the fun.

own fireworks; they shot firecrackers in any direction, blew up tin cans, or threw "torpedos" against the wall to watch the gunpowder explode. But every city that had any money in the treasury staged a fireworks show—which was often held on the water to double the effect. Almost the whole town piled into the park, to watch the show in the sky, while a band played in the gazebo. The band always saved "The Star Spangled Banner" for last, and everyone trudged home, with those notes ringing in their heads.

America, however, has had more than one Independence Day. Just as the Colonies commemorate emancipation from England on July 4, African-Americans have also celebrated emancipation from slavery on June 19. Called Juneteenth, the happy day has been observed by African-Americans for over a century. It marks the day when General Gordon Granger spread the news of the Emancipation Proclamation to Texas and Louisiana. Blacks who left brought the festival with them to other states—Arkansas, Colorado, Oklahoma. With a band, and a big cookout, featuring a pit barbecue or some other special food, Juneteenth parallels the Fourth, with a few significant differences: parade floats celebrate freedom, and a Miss Juneteenth, crowned and caped, becomes the honorary monarch of the day. In many communities, teams formed to clean up the cemetery and local countryside. After it was all

Flags hung out for the Fourth.

over, everyone could still look forward to the Fourth of July.

The party of the summer, the Jubilee on the Fourth always opened the season officially. After that, Americans took weekends off, went on vacation, got out the sailboat, went fishing, got out of town, and played like children until Labor Day.

Opposite: The Fourth of July brought out the whole neighborhood to celebrate the Declaration of Independence. In 1961 on this Chicago street, patriotic residents posed under a foliage of flags.

ACKNOWLEDGMENTS

126

All photographs are by Dudley Witney with the exception of the following:

Albright-Knox Art Gallery, Buffalo, N.Y., Charles Clifton and James G. Forsyth Funds, for Winslow Homer, *Croquet Players*, 1865, oil on canvas, 16 x 26", 95

Henry Ford Museum & Greenfield Village, from *Americans on Vacation*, 13, 16, 21, 46, 51

The Library of Congress, 7, 10, 12, 17, 20, 24, 25, 30, 32, 34, 39, 48, 49, 50, 52, 54, 56, 59, 60, 62, 63, 64, 66, 68, 71, 72, 74, 76, 85, 89, 92, 94, 96, 97, 99, 100, 102, 106, 107, 108, 109, 110, 112, 115, 117, 118, 121, 122, 123

National Archives, 53, 55, 67, 91, 119, 125

INDEX

*Faded blue jeans dry in
the summer sun.*

128